the Country Friends® Collection

Merry Mixes

Holly
... looks year-'round for wonderful ribbons & trims.

Kate
... wonders if she dropped the nutmeg can lid in the Merry Mix.

Mary Elizabeth
... loves to deliver her Merry Mixes!

TeA

SPICY WINTER TEA MIX

a recipe from Patti Davis ★ Kiowa, OK

- 1·¼ c. orange drink mix
- 3/4 c. sweetened instant tea
- ½ t. ground cloves
- ½ t. allspice
- .23-oz. pkg. lemonade drink mix
- 1 t. cinnamon
- 3-oz. pkg. apricot gelatin
- 9-oz. pkg. red cinnamon candies

Combine all ingredients together and store in an airtight container. Makes about 3·½ cups dry mix.

☆ A Packaging Idea! ☆

Visit your neighborhood craft store for a stack of small clay pots ∿ they're great country·style containers that, with a coat of paint, will carry your tea mix with down·home flair. Simply paint the pots a dark red or forest green; rub a bit of the color off with fine sandpaper when dry. Stencil a star and the word "TEA" on the pots, or use rubber stamps to decorate the pots. Package the tea mix in plastic zipping bags and gather a piece of muslin or plaid homespun fabric around the mix ∿ tie shut with raffia or jute and place in the painted pots. Add directions!

SPICY ☆ Winter Tea Mix

Warm up a cold winter day! Add 3 heaping tablespoons of mix to one cup of hot water. Stir and sip!

↑ Feel free to make copies of this tag! Color it up as you wish!

SPICY TeA MIX

TeA

Doing good is the only certainly HAPPY action of a man's Life.

—SIR PHILLIP SIDNEY—

Cheery Cherry Tea

a recipe from Michelle Campen
* Peoria, IL

Sew a pretty fabric bag for your cherry tea mix gifts!

Simply cut a piece of fabric (A CHERRY PRINT WOULD BE FUN!) with pinking shears; fold in half, right-side out, and stitch the sides together.

FOLD HERE

Slip a plastic bag of tea mix inside and tie the bag shut with a wide satin ribbon. Tie on these directions:

CHEERY CHERRY
T E A

Stir 1 to 2 tablespoons of tea mix in one cup of hot or cold water.

15-oz. jar orange drink mix
1 c. sugar
1 c. unsweetened instant tea
½ c. lemonade powder
0.13-oz. pkg. cherry drink mix
2 t. cinnamon
1 t. nutmeg

Blend all ingredients together well and store in an airtight container. Makes about 5 cups of dry mix.

Pepperminty Cocoa

a good idea from Jen Sell ★ Farmington, MN

3 c. powdered milk
1·¼ c. sugar
½ c. baking cocoa
8 to 10 peppermint
    candies, crushed
⅛ t. salt

Stir all ingredients together and store in a wide-mouth, one-quart canning jar or airtight container.

Make a cute and yummy gift! Glue a whole, round peppermint on top of the jar lid... tie a scrap of red and white homespun 'round the jar neck and slip a candy cane in the knot. Don't forget to glue a copy of the instructions below on the jar!

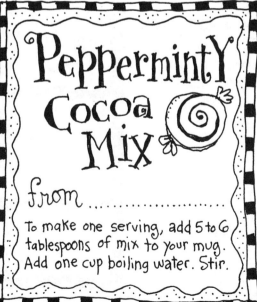

Pepperminty Cocoa Mix

from ....

To make one serving, add 5 to 6 tablespoons of mix to your mug. Add one cup boiling water. Stir.

This recipe reminds me of one my mother fixes when the weather turns nippy!

Make a nostalgia trip out of this gift: pack the mix in a mason jar and wrap it in a flour-sack kind of towel ~ the kind your mom used to use! Hand-write the instructions on a recipe card and pop it and the towel & mix in an old-fashioned, clear-glass measuring bowl. Tie on a rick-rack bow!

Snowy ❄ Morning ❄ Waffle Mix ❄

a recipe from Annmarie Aquino ★ New York, NY

2 T. brown sugar, packed	3 c. whole-wheat flour
2 t. baking powder	1 c. cornmeal
1 t. baking soda	

Mix ingredients to blend and store in an airtight container. Makes about 4 cups of waffle mix.

Attach these instructions to your gift tag:
Separate 4 eggs. Beat yolks with ⅓ cup oil and 3 cups of buttermilk; add waffle mix, blending 'til smooth. Beat egg whites until stiff; fold into waffle batter. Pour on greased waffle iron - bake until steaming stops.

MY FAVORITE PANCAKES!

a really good & fruity recipe from Jojo Santos-Harmon
* Villa Hills, KY

Everybody has a favorite, and this mix will be yours!

- 1 c. all-purpose flour
- 1 T. brown sugar, packed
- 2 t. baking powder
- ¼ t. salt
- ½ t. cinnamon

Mix all ingredients well. Store in airtight tin or one-pint canning jar.

Make copies of the label below and glue to plain old lunch sacks. Seal mix in plastic zipping bags and drop in lunch sacks. Fold over sack tops ~ tie shut with a ribbon!

♥ MY FAVORITE ♥ PANCAKE ♥
— MIX —
in the whole, wide, wonderful world!
♥ from _____ ♥

Pour pancake mix in large bowl; make a well in the center. Add ¼ teaspoon vanilla extract, 1 beaten egg, 1 cup milk & 2 tablespoons oil ~ blend thoroughly. Stir in ½ cup applesauce. Spoon ¼ cup batter on a hot, greased griddle or skillet. Cook until bubbles form around edges, then turn. Makes 8-10 pancakes.

Mornin' Sunshine Syrup Mix

a recipe from Vickie *
Gooseberry Patch

¼ c. brown sugar, packed   ¼ t. allspice
2 T. cornstarch   ⅛ t. nutmeg

Stir dry ingredients together and store in airtight tin.

This syrup is terrific over pancakes and waffles!
For gift-giving, make copies of this sunny-faced tag on bright yellow paper. Write these instructions on the back of the tag and tie on with a yellow gingham ribbon!

"Add dry ingredients to a saucepan and stir in 1¾ cups apple cider. Cook over medium heat until mixture begins to thicken and is bubbly."

Makes 1¾ cups syrup.

Mornin' Sunshine Syrup Mix from

Snowflake Muffin Mix

a 'specially yummy recipe from
Linda Hensz ✳ Beach Lake, PA

These are oh-so-fragrant and good on a snowy day! Pack a disposable plastic container with this mix...tie on a paper snowflake with a blue satin ribbon, pull on your snowboots and deliver to a friendly neighbor!

2 c. all-purpose flour
1 T. dry onion soup mix
1½ T. sugar

2 t. baking powder
½ t. baking soda
¼ t. salt

Measure ingredients in a medium mixing bowl; stir and store in an airtight container. Give with a copy of the following directions:

POUR MIX IN LARGE MIXING BOWL and MAKE A WELL IN CENTER OF DRY INGREDIENTS. BEAT TOGETHER ONE EGG, ⅓ CUP OIL, ONE CUP SHREDDED SHARP CHEDDAR CHEESE & ONE CUP MILK. COMBINE WITH MIX; STIR TO MOISTEN. FILL 12 GREASED MUFFIN CUPS 3/4 FULL. BAKE AT 400 DEGREES FOR 15 TO 20 MINUTES. COOL 5 MINUTES, THEN REMOVE FROM MUFFIN TINS. MAKES ONE DOZEN MUFFINS.

Snow flake Muffin Mix

Give,

and it shall be given unto you; **good measure,** pressed down, and shaken together, and **running over.**

-New Testament, Luke 6:38-

Homemade CREAM SOUP MIX

something delicious from
ALANA FOLLAS ★ BELEWS CREEK, NC

2 c. powdered milk
¼ c. beef, chicken or vegetable bouillon granules
2 T. dried onion flakes
1 t. dried basil
1 t. dried thyme
½ t. pepper
¾ c. cornstarch

Mix all ingredients together until well blended. Store in airtight container or plastic zipping bag.

YUM

GIVING DOESN'T ONLY WORK AT HOLIDAY TIME; MAKE A SPECIAL DELIVERY OUT·OF·THE·BLUE, FOR NO SPECIAL OCCASION, TO REALLY MAKE SOMEONE'S DAY.

To use in place of canned cream soup in your favorite casserole, combine 1/3 cup of soup mix with 1-1/4 cups of cold water in a saucepan. Cook over medium heat until thickened.

← Here are the directions for using the soup mix... copy it and glue it on the can's backside. Color the labels as you wish!

★ Glue a photo of your smiling face in the circle... color copy and use it as your new front label!

clean out tin cans and remove the labels...use sandpaper to remove any sharp edges, then glue on your personalized wrapper! Drop a bag of mix in for a clever and tasty gift.

your face goes here!

YUM YUM

My Home·made·Good Cream Soup Mix!

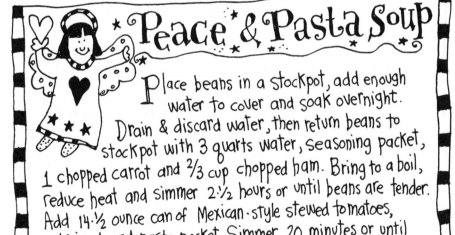

¾ c. dried onion flakes
3 T. dried basil
3 T. dried oregano
2 t. garlic powder
2 2.¼ oz. jars beef
    bouillon granules

2 c. dried black-eyed peas
2 c. dried black beans
2 c. dried navy beans
2 c. dried kidney beans
16-oz. pkg. small shell pasta,
    uncooked

Blend first 5 ingredients together and divide in 6 plastic zipping bags ~ add a tag that says "SEASONING PACKET". Combine peas & beans; divide in 6 plastic zipping bags or airtight containers. Divide pasta among 6 airtight containers. To give as a gift, tuck one of each of the seasoning, bean and pasta packages in a basket or colander with these directions:

Peace & Pasta Soup

Place beans in a stockpot, add enough water to cover and soak overnight. Drain & discard water, then return beans to stockpot with 3 quarts water, seasoning packet, 1 chopped carrot and ⅔ cup chopped ham. Bring to a boil, reduce heat and simmer 2½ hours or until beans are tender. Add 14½ ounce can of Mexican-style stewed tomatoes, undrained, and pasta packet. Simmer 20 minutes or until pasta is done. Makes 9 servings of delicious soup!

There are 2 worlds; the world that we can measure with line and rule, and the world that we feel with our hearts and imagination.
— Leigh Hunt

an oh-so-good recipe from
Linda Manning ★ Noxapater, MS

Make 10 gifts from this recipe ....
but keep one for yourself!

CRAZY QUILT BEAN SOUP MIX

1 lb. pearl barley
1 lb. dried black beans
1 lb. dried red beans
1 lb. dried pinto beans
1 lb. dried navy beans
1 lb. dried Great Northern beans
1 lb. dried lentils
1 lb. dried split peas
1 lb. dried black-eyed peas

Mix together all beans and divide into 10 one-pint canning jars for gift giving. Tie on a recipe card with the directions shown on adjacent page!

Gratitude is heaven itself; there could be no heaven without gratitude; I feel it and I know it. I thank God and man for it. — William Blake

May
the faith that gives us
HOPE,
may the Love
that shows the way,
may the PEACE
that cheers the heart,
be
Yours
this day.
-anonymous-

You can copy this card on red paper ~ tie on with a green ribbon! Pretty!

● How to Make a Yummy Pot of CRAZY QUILT BEAN SOUP:

Add beans to a Dutch oven, add enough water to cover and soak overnight. Drain beans and discard water, then return beans to Dutch oven. Add 2 quarts water, 1 pound diced ham, 1 clove minced garlic and ½ teaspoon salt. Cover and bring to a boil, then reduce heat and simmer 1·½ hours or 'til beans are tender. Add 16·ounce can undrained tomatoes & 10·ounce can tomatoes with chopped chilies. Simmer 30 minutes longer. Makes 8 to 10 servings.

Wild West Steak Rub

a ZIPPY RECIPE FROM MERRILL POWERS ★ SPEARVILLE, KS

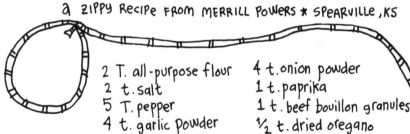

2 T. all-purpose flour	4 t. onion powder
2 t. salt	1 t. paprika
5 T. pepper	1 t. beef bouillon granules
4 t. garlic powder	½ t. dried oregano

Mix all ingredients together — store in a plastic zipping bag or airtight container. Makes about ½ cup. Give with these directions:

WILD ★ WEST STEAK RUB

SPRINKLE DESIRED AMOUNT OVER STEAKS, THEN REFRIGERATE MEAT AT LEAST 4 HOURS TO ALLOW THE FLAVORS TO BLEND. GRILL STEAKS TO DESIRED DONENESS. ENJOY!

← You are welcome to make a copy of our tag, ma'am!

★IDEA!

GATHER UP A RED COTTON BANDANA 'ROUND A PACKET OF STEAK RUB AND TIE IT SHUT WITH A LASSO OF JUTE. TIE ON A GIFT TAG & GIVE IT ALONG WITH A GIFT CERTIFICATE FOR A GOOD, THICK STEAK AT YOUR LOCAL MEAT MARKET.

Tasty Herb Mix

a recipe from
April Jacobs
Loveland, Co

⅓ c. dry milk   1 ½ t. dried thyme
1 T. salt   1 t. onion powder
1 T. paprika   1 t. dill weed
2 t. dry mustard   ½ t. garlic powder
2 t. dried oregano   ¼ t. pepper

Add all ingredients together in a one-cup jar with lid ~ shake well. Makes ⅔ cup mix. Tie on a recipe card or copy of these recipes:

Tasty Herb Mix

FOR DELICIOUS CRUNCHY FRIED CHICKEN, COMBINE 4 TABLESPOONS OF HERB MIX WITH 6 TABLESPOONS OF FLOUR. COAT 2 TO 3 POUNDS OF CHICKEN. BROWN CHICKEN IN 2 TABLESPOONS OF OIL FOR 15 MINUTES ON EACH SIDE OR UNTIL JUICES RUN CLEAR.

from the Kitchen of

★Pack this tasty mix in something fun! A clear glass SUGAR SHAKER from the discount store would be neat... pour the mix in, then lay a square of clear plastic wrap over the jar top to seal out moisture. Before you screw the lid on, add a piece of thin cotton homespun over the top... now tighten that lid! ★Another good packaging idea: how about an old-fashioned graniteware salt shaker?

Jingle Bells Chili Mix

a recipe from Nancy Machcinski ★ Erlanger, KY

Here's a silly way to give a tasty chili gift! Make a batch of this dry chili mix and spoon it into plastic zipping bags. Now make a neat envelope to hide the plastic bag inside! Find an old sheet of music ⌣ one without words, just with musical notes ⌣ and fold it in half. Glue the sides together and leave the top open so you can slip the chili mix bag inside.

(open end)

Glue this side shut.

Glue this side shut.

(Fold)

Okay, now make a copy of our SILLY CHILI MUSICAL TAG (shown on adjacent page →) and attach it to your envelope full of chili mix with a ribbon and a jingle bell; tie the envelope shut. You're good to go!

FA ★ LA ★ LA ★ LA ★

JINGLE BELLS CHILI MIX TASTY ALL THE WAY OH'! WHAT FUN TO EAT ON AN OH SO CHILI DAY!

COUNTRY FRIENDS CHOIR

On the subject of singing: the frog school and the lark school disagree. — chinese proverb

RECIPE FOR CHILI MIX:

1·¼ t. cinnamon
1·¼ t. cumin
1·½ t. cayenne pepper
4 T. chili powder
1·¼ t. allspice

1 T. salt
4 bay leaves
½ t. garlic salt
4 T. dried onion

Combine all ingredients and spoon into a plastic zipping bag.

Jingle Bells Chili Mix, Tasty all the way, Oh! What fun it is to eat on an OH·so·chili day!

from the kitchen of _____

Fix a batch of this good chili simply by blending chili mix with 2·½ pounds browned ground beef, 1½ quarts water, 12·oz. can tomato paste, 1·¼ tablespoons vinegar and 1 tablespoon Worcestershire sauce in a stockpot. Simmer 4 hours. Enjoy in a bowl or spoon over prepared spaghetti. Garnish with onions and cheese. Makes 6 to 8 servings.

Here's your instruction tag to copy & tie on!

from our
Holiday
House
to
yours

coconut
Brownie
Mix

merry
christmas
from

COCONUT Brownie Mix

an easy recipe from Carol Weimer
★ Saltsburg, PA

- ⅓ c. CHOPPED WALNUTS
- ½ c. CHOCOLATE CHIPS
- ⅓ c. COCONUT
- ⅔ c. BROWN SUGAR, packed
- 3/4 c. SUGAR
- ⅓ c. BAKING COCOA
- 1·½ c. ALL-PURPOSE FLOUR

★

Layer ingredients in a wide-mouth, one-quart canning jar. Pack each layer down as tightly as possible before adding the next layer.

★

← Make a copy of this tag ... color it up ... then handwrite the following instructions on the back:

Add mix to 2 eggs, ⅔ cup oil, 1 teaspoon vanilla extract. Blend well. Spread in greased 8" baking dish. Bake at 350 degrees for 30 minutes or 'til center tests done. Makes 12 brownies.

Merry Mixes
Unforgettable Gift Wrappings

☆ BAKE A BATCH OF GIFT TAGS! That's right— baked shortbread stars with a hole poked in the middle can be strung on a piece of jute and tied on a simple kraft box for a primitive Christmas country wrap! Just pop your Merry Mix in the box and make a special delivery.

OLD HANKIES, ☆ HATBOXES, GALVANIZED BUCKETS, OLD KITCHEN MOLDS & PANS, SAP BUCKETS, VINTAGE CIGAR BOXES... unexpected and clever containers for Merry Mixes!

☆ BEAUTIFUL OLD POSTCARDS at flea markets can be picked up for a dollar or two... and the illustrations are charming. Look for Christmas designs that are blank on the backside ⌣ write your Merry Mix directions on it, and tie to your gift for lovely old-fashioned sharing!

Knock·knock.
—— WHO'S THERE ? ——
orange. —ORANGE WHO?—
Orange you glad
I'm bringing you a MERRY MIX ?

North Pole Cookie Bar Mix

...a little elf's favorite!

a recipe from Zoe Bennett Columbia, SC

½ C. QUICK-COOKING OATS, UNCOOKED
½ C. RASPBERRY CHIPS
1 C. BROWN SUGAR, PACKED & DIVIDED

2 C. BUTTERMILK BISCUIT BAKING MIX, DIVIDED

— ★ —

In a wide-mouth, one-quart glass jar, layer ingredients in this order: OATS, RASPBERRY CHIPS, ½ CUP BROWN SUGAR, ONE CUP BUTTERMILK BISCUIT BAKING MIX, ½ CUP BROWN SUGAR AND ONE CUP BUTTERMILK BISCUIT BAKING MIX. Pack layers in jar tightly, and if there's room left, add more chips to top of jar. Give with these instructions:

from the little elves in the _____ kitchen:

NORTH ★ POLE ★ COOKIE ★ BARS

Combine jar mix with ½ cup melted butter, one egg and one teaspoon vanilla extract; blend well. Press cookie mix in a greased 8" baking dish ∽ bake at 350 degrees for 18 to 22 minutes or until golden and almost set. Makes 16 bars ∽ enough for you and your little elves!

Chewy Bars in a Jar MIX

...Heavenly!

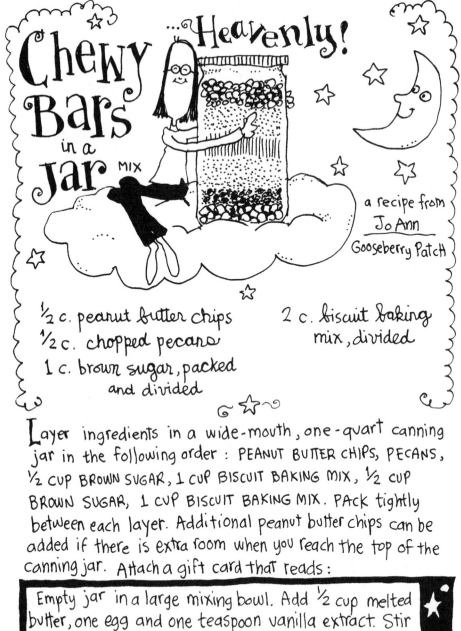

a recipe from
Jo Ann
Gooseberry Patch

½ c. peanut butter chips
½ c. chopped pecans
1 c. brown sugar, packed and divided

2 c. biscuit baking mix, divided

Layer ingredients in a wide-mouth, one-quart canning jar in the following order: PEANUT BUTTER CHIPS, PECANS, ½ CUP BROWN SUGAR, 1 CUP BISCUIT BAKING MIX, ½ CUP BROWN SUGAR, 1 CUP BISCUIT BAKING MIX. PACK tightly between each layer. Additional peanut butter chips can be added if there is extra room when you reach the top of the canning jar. Attach a gift card that reads:

Empty jar in a large mixing bowl. Add ½ cup melted butter, one egg and one teaspoon vanilla extract. Stir to blend, then press into an 8" greased baking dish. Bake at 350 degrees for 18 to 20 minutes or 'til golden. Makes 18 bars. Enjoy with a big glass of cold milk!

Chewy Bars in A Jar

WoW...wish I'd thought of that!

good IdeAs!

★ Take a stroll through the craft store ⌁ paper-edger scissors and paper punches come in all sorts of FUN designs! Punch snowflakes all around the top of a white shopping bag...cut a fancy scalloped edge on a lunch bag... play dress-up with wrappers for your Merry Mixes!

★ Vintage is IN! Visit flea markets & tag sales and gather up an armload of jars, old tin canisters, flour sifters & colanders to hold your mixes.

★ Draw a simple holiday design on a heavy card or tag ⌁ maybe a star? Then simply perforate holes in the outline of the design and connect the dots ... with bright red yarn in a fat needle!

What a fun handmade tag!

Kate
from Holly

Wisdom is the principal thing; therefore get wisdom: and with all thy getting get understanding. — Old Testament, Proverbs 4:7

TAGS

FOR MERRY MIXES

... JUST COPY, CUT & COLOR!

Do Not Open 'Til Christmas

to: _____

from: _____

merry CHRISTMAS

To: From:

Oh Joy! It's CHristmas!

a little gift from ....

for ....

White Christmas Pumpkin Bread

a recipe from Gail Masters ✹ Belton, MO

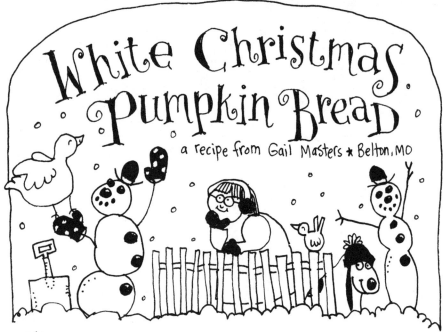

- 1.½ c. SUGAR
- 1 t. BAKING SODA
- ¼ t. BAKING POWDER
- ½ t. GROUND CLOVES
- ½ t. CINNAMON
- ½ t. SALT
- ½ t. NUTMEG
- 1.2/3 c. ALL-PURPOSE FLOUR

WHISK TOGETHER INGREDIENTS TO THOROUGHLY BLEND; SPOON INTO PLASTIC ZIPPING BAGS.

INCLUDE A COPY OF THESE DIRECTIONS WITH THE MIX:

White Christmas Pumpkin Bread

To prepare, blend mix with ½ cup oil, ½ cup water, one cup canned pumpkin and two beaten eggs. Spread in a greased 9" x 5" loaf pan and bake at 350 degrees for one hour. Makes 6 servings.

My Favorite Bread... My Favorite Time of Year! from............

GIVING ☆Ideas:

GIVE YOUR GIFT TAGS & RECIPE DIRECTION CARDS A HOLIDAY SPARKLE... GLUE A SPRINKLE OF **GLITTER** IN THE CORNERS OF TAGS & CARDS WITH EASY-TO-USE SPRAY ADHESIVE. CLEAR CRYSTAL GLITTER IS PRETTY, PRETTY, PRETTY.

(HEY, GLITTER UP THAT TOTE BAG, TOO!)

A WHITE PAPER TOTE BAG WITH A RECIPE CARD GLUED ON THE FRONT WILL HOLD A MERRY MIX... JUST ADD A PIECE OF WHITE TISSUE & A CASCADE OF WHITE CURLING RIBBONS...

a *wonderful* **WHITE** *Christmas gift.*

Think Snowy White:

A WHITE MIXING BOWL LINED WITH A SNOWY-WHITE TOWEL OR DOILY... A CLEAR BAG FULL OF WHITE CHRISTMAS PUMPKIN BREAD MIX... A WHITE RIBBON & CLUSTER OF WHITE BERRIES... A CLASSIC!

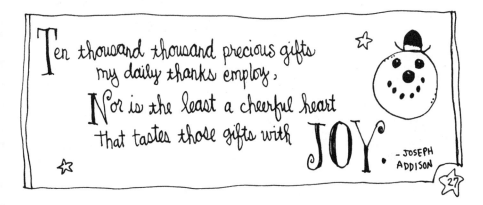

Ten thousand thousand precious gifts
my daily thanks employ,
Nor is the least a cheerful heart
that tastes those gifts with **JOY.**

— JOSEPH ADDISON

27

Easy Cinnamon Roll Mix

a recipe from
Stacie Ramon
Tonasket, WA

18-¼ oz. box yellow cake mix

5 c. all-purpose flour

2 T. instant yeast

Stir all ingredients together and store in an airtight container. Give with a copy of these directions:

Easy Cinnamon Rolls ...to make, bake & eat.

Combine mix with 2·½ cups hot water. Stir well and let rise in a warm place until double in size. Punch down dough, roll in a 15" x 10" rectangle. Spread dough with ¼ cup melted butter, then sprinkle 2 tablespoons cinnamon and 3/4 cup sugar evenly over top. Roll dough jelly roll-style ~ slice in 18 equal size rolls. Divide rolls between 2 greased 13" x 9" baking dishes and let rise again until double. Bake at 350 degrees for 25 to 30 minutes or until golden.

from the kitchen of _____

OH! Pretty Packaging!

Have a rubber stamp made with your initial on it ∼ a big one! Stamp it on white lunch bags, totes, flour sack towels... use a different color ink every year for "signature" gift wrap!

Sometimes simple trims make the prettiest packages. Look to nature for neat stuff to tie on your gift packs ∼ a sprig of evergreen, one single holly leaf, a beautifully textured twig ∼ and attach with jute or raffia bows. A dab of hot glue will help hold everything in place.

Check out antique shops and tag sales for vintage tablecloths and kitchen linens... a little tatter here and there won't hurt! You can cut worn places out of old pieces and use the beautifully patterned fabric to make lovely gift bags for your Merry Mixes. Tie with a piece of rick-rack for a charming retro look!

Merry Mixes from little hands

Here are three **FUN** recipes for kids in the kitchen... easy to make, and not a one has to be precise... so what if Frosty's Toppers is 99% gumdrops? Your little elves will have a holiday blast mixing up gifts for neighbors, Aunt Helen and the mailman, too. So get out the crayons, color the tags and get mixin'!

reindeer treats

Reindeer need their veggies, too, you know!

*

1 bag of pre-washed BABY CARROTS

1 head of cauliflower, divided into florets

*

Your little elf can mix up a plastic bag of carrots & cauliflower, and tie it shut with a copy of this tag and a wide holiday ribbon! Deliver to every neighbor's house where Rudolph stops by!

Frosty's Toppers

For vanilla ice cream!

Use your imagination... Fill a plastic bag with all kinds of yummy little candies to top off vanilla ice cream!

★

Multicolored candy sprinkles   Peanuts

Non-pareils   Coconut

Small candies

Red & Green Gumdrops

Mini Marshmallows

★

Pour all ingredients into a mixing bowl. Your child can stir it up and use a tablespoon to dump it into individual bags. Tie with curling ribbon & a tag!

★ FEEL FREE TO MAKE COPIES OF OUR TAGS for YOUR KIDS TO COLOR.

Yum! Santa will love this pretty sugar for his tea or cereal!

★

Mix together one cup of sugar with red- and green-colored sugars...the kind you shake on cookies. Throw in a bunch of star-shaped cookie sprinkles, too, for fun! Divide into individual small plastic bags; add a tag & ribbon.

Santa Sugar

Merry Mixes II

Index

One of the very nicest things about life is the way we must regularly stop whatever it is we are doing and devote our attention to EATING. — LUCIANO PAVAROTTI